Barbie
ANNUAL 2026

First published in Great Britain 2025 by Farshore
An imprint of HarperCollins*Publishers*
1 London Bridge Street, London SE1 9GF
www.farshore.co.uk

HarperCollins*Publishers*
Macken House, 39/40 Mayor Street Upper,
Dublin 1, D01 C9W8, Ireland

Written by Caroline Rowlands

ISBN 978 0 00 868214 9
Printed in Romania
001

A CIP catalogue record for this title is available from the British Library.

Adult supervision is advised for all craft and colouring activities. Always ask an adult to help when
using glue, paint and scissors. Wear protective clothing and cover surfaces to avoid staining.

Adult supervision is recommended when using any kitchen
equipment including ovens and other heat sources.

Stay safe online. Farshore is not responsible for content hosted by third parties.

MIX
Paper | Supporting
responsible forestry
FSC™ C007454

This book contains FSC™ certified paper and other controlled
sources to ensure responsible forest management.

For more information visit: www.harpercollins.co.uk/green

This Annual belongs to:

_____

Age:

_____

Contents

We Dream Together

Say hi to Brooklyn and Malibu! When these fearless friends join forces, the sky is the limit!

FRIENDS MAKE THE WORLD A BETTER PLACE!

BROOKLYN

Name: Barbie 'Brooklyn' Roberts

Lives: New York

Family: Simone and Kel (mum and dad) and Viola (grandmother)

BFFs: Malibu and Rafa Gonzalez

Likes: songwriting, playing guitar, dancing and writing in her journal

Personality: adventurous, optimistic, fearless and loyal

Pet: Etta the cat

Dreams of ... achieving the impossible!

BROOKLYN WAS BORN TO DANCE!

MALIBU IS A TRUE GOAL GETTER!

TOGETHER WE SHINE!

MALIBU

Name: Barbie 'Malibu' Roberts

Lives: California and New York

Family: Margaret and George (mum and dad), Skipper, Stacie and Chelsea (sisters)

BFFs: Brooklyn, Ken, Teresa, Renee, Nikki and Daisy

Likes: music, vlogging, fashion and animals

Personality: energetic, curious and kind

Pet: Taffy the puppy and Blissa the cat

Dreams of ... being her own authentic, amazing self!

FUR-EVER FRIENDS!

Dream Big

When you have big dreams you can achieve anything! Take this fun quiz to discover your future career.

1

What do you like doing most at school?

a. Drawing and crafts

b. Reading and writing

c. Counting and sums

2

Which outing would be your perfect day trip?

a. Exploring an art gallery or museum

b. Visiting a wildlife park

c. Riding a rollercoaster in a theme park

3

Which gift is top of your wish list?

a. Painting set

b. Cuddly toy

c. Telescope

WRITE IN THE NAMES OF THREE OF YOUR FRIENDS, THEN FOLLOW THE LINES TO REVEAL WHAT THEY MIGHT BECOME.

CHEF

PILOT

MUSICIAN

....

....

....

4
Which word sums you up best?
a. Creative
b. Caring
c. Adventurous

5
What kind of movies do you like?
a. Animated movies
b. Funny movies
c. Exciting movies

6
Which type of transport do you like the most?
a. Bike
b. Car
c. Aeroplane

7
During your free time you like to ...
a. Draw a picture
b. Play in the park
c. Bounce on a trampoline

How did you score?

MOSTLY a ...
Your creative and artistic skills are suited to a career as a make-up artist, games creator, chef or fashion designer.

MOSTLY b ...
Your kind and caring nature would make you a brilliant vet, doctor or teacher.

MOSTLY c ...
Your adventurous spirit will take you far. Aim high and become a pilot, firefighter or astronaut.

Style Spotter!

Can you spot 5 differences between these pictures of Brooklyn and Malibu?

a

b

Answers on page 69.

TOO EASY? Now try and find 8 differences between these pictures.

1

2

Mystery Shopping

Malibu and Brooklyn are going shopping! Can you crack the code to reveal what they have bought on their shopping trip?

a _ _ _ _ _ _ _ _ _ _

b _ _ _ _ _ _ _ _

c _ _ _ _ _ _ _ _

d _ _ _ _ _ _ _ _ _

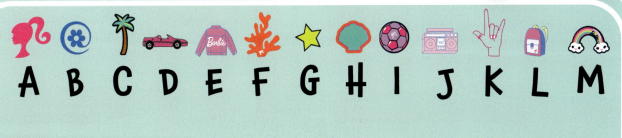

A B C D E F G H I J K L M

N O P Q R S T U V W X Y Z

Answers on page 69.

Barbie A TOUCH OF MAGIC

YOU CAN DRIVE my car

1

"Working at the water park is the best!"

Brooklyn really wanted a job at the water park. First, she needed to pass her driving test. She had never failed a test in her life!

2

"How about I help you practice?"

To her surprise, Brooklyn failed the test. Malibu tried to cheer her up and offered to help Brooklyn practice driving.

3

"This is not working …"

But Malibu was nervous and she kept telling Brooklyn to brake. "You're so nervous, it's making me nervous," said Brooklyn, before she stopped the car.

4

"Hmmm, I guess so …"

Later, Brooklyn went home to tell her mum about her test. "Do you want me to help?" her mum asked. "I do teach pilots to fly jumbo jets …"

5

Brooklyn's mum was nervous, too! She made Brooklyn complete a pre-drive checklist before starting the lesson.

6

Brooklyn went to talk to Malibu. "My mum didn't even let me start the car," sighed Brooklyn. "I'll never pass."

7

Malibu's mum overheard them. "I'd be happy to take you for a spin," she said. "Great idea!" cried Malibu. "Mum is an amazing teacher! She never gets nervous."

8

Meanwhile, Malibu's sisters were tying balloons to Chelsea to see how many it took to lift her off the ground. They wanted to help their friend Peggy, the pegasus, fly back home.

9

During the driving lesson, Brooklyn was stuck in traffic. Peggy woke up from a nap in the back seat and heard Brooklyn say, "I wish this car could fly!"

10

Suddenly, magic sparkled and the car lifted off. "Is this car flying?" asked Malibu's mum, trying to sound calm as they flew over rooftops.

15

11

Brooklyn pulled the car out of a nosedive to save them from landing in the water! "I can do this!" she told herself. Just then, Peggy cast another spell, sending Malibu's mum to sleep. With this, Brooklyn called Malibu using the hands-free button on the steering wheel.

12

Malibu couldn't believe her ears when Brooklyn told her she was flying. "Don't panic, Brooklyn. I know you can handle this," she told her calmly.

13

Brooklyn felt better already. "I think I'm getting the hang of it, Malibu!" she replied. "Woah. I think ... Can you send us some kind of signal so I can find our street?"

14

Malibu quickly came up with a plan to get Brooklyn back home. She went into the front garden with her sisters and attached the huge bunch of balloons to a long rope. Then they secured it safely to the ground.

On Malibu's signal, Skipper loosened the rope and the balloons flew up. Luckily, Brooklyn saw this and drove towards it.

16 *Wow! That was awesome, Brooklyn!*

In no time, Brooklyn smoothly landed the car and parked it on the driveway. Just then, Malibu's mum woke up.

You passed! Well done.

Congratulations!

The next day, Brooklyn passed her test. "Water park job, here I come!" said Brooklyn.

18

Brooklyn and Malibu hopped straight in the car, but after all her hard work, Brooklyn decided she wanted a job she could walk to instead. So she decided to apply for the Selfie Museum ... and she got the job!

THE END

Better Together

Choose a friend to play this friendship game with. Each fill in a panel, without the other seeing. Then compare your answers and see how many are the same.

NAME _____ AGE ____

The song we sing together most:

_____

The song we love to dance to:

_____

Our favourite singer:

_____

Our favourite movie:

_____

Funniest thing we've done:

_____

Best day out together:

_____

Our favourite book:

_____

How we cheer each other up:

_____

Who we admire most:

_____

NAME _____ AGE ____

The song we sing together most:

_____

The song we love to dance to:

_____

Our favourite singer:

_____

Our favourite movie:

_____

Funniest thing we've done:

_____

Best day out together:

_____

Our favourite book:

_____

How we cheer each other up:

_____

Who we admire most:

_____

GROUP CHAT!

Tell Brooklyn and Malibu your favourite things to do with friends.

18

Team Barbie

Can you work out which pieces go where to complete this picture?

Sleepover Squad

Malibu and Brooklyn are having a sleepover and all their friends are invited! Help each friend find their way through the maze so they can join in the fun.

RENEE

NIKK

FINISH

DAISY

GROUP CHAT!

Have you ever been to a sleepover?

Answers on page 69.

Party Planner

Follow the simple steps below to plan the perfect sleepover party for you and your friends.

GIVE YOUR PARTY A THEME. PICK ONE FROM THE LIST BELOW OR MAKE UP YOUR OWN.

☐ Movie marathon
☐ Dance party
☐ Makeover magic
☐ Craft party

WRITE A GUEST LIST AND SEND OUT YOUR INVITES A COUPLE OF WEEKS BEFORE.

....
....
....
....

TRY OUT THIS AWESOME PARTY GAME AT YOUR SLEEPOVER!

SARDINES

One player hides and the rest hunt for them. Whoever finds the hidden player then has to hide with them (and is the winner). Play until there is only one hunter left.

MAKE SURE YOU HAVE EVERYTHING READY, BEFORE YOUR GUESTS ARRIVE.

☐ Snacks
☐ Drinks
☐ Pillows
☐ Blankets/ sleeping bags
☐ Board games
☐ Music playlist
☐ Movies to watch

☐ Cute pyjamas
☐ Cosy socks
☐ Fluffy slippers
☐ Eye masks
☐ Torches
☐ (Any other items linked to your theme e.g. crafts to make)

Get Your Bake On!

Follow the steps below to make these sweet treats for your friends or family.

CHOC CHIP COOKIES

WHAT YOU NEED

- 130g butter (softened)
- 100g caster sugar
- 100g light soft brown sugar
- 1 egg
- 1 tsp vanilla essence
- 180g plain flour or gluten-free flour
- ½ tsp bicarbonate of soda
- ½ tsp baking powder
- 100g milk chocolate chips

NEED DAIRY-FREE? Use dairy-free butter and chocolate chips.

WHAT YOU DO

1. Preheat the oven to 190°C/170°C fan/ gas mark 5.
2. Mix the butter, caster sugar and brown sugar together until soft and well combined.
3. Add the egg and vanilla essence and mix to combine.
4. Next add the flour, bicarbonate of soda and baking powder and mix well.
5. Finally, sprinkle in the chocolate chips and combine them with your mixture.
6. Line baking trays with greaseproof paper. Take 2 teaspoons of mixture and add to the tray – making sure each dough ball is 5cm apart. You will have enough dough to make 30 cookies.
7. Ask an adult to bake your cookies for 10 to 12 minutes, or until golden, and leave to cool. Yum!

FRUIT FLOWERS

WHAT YOU NEED

- 250g cream cheese
- 6 rice cakes
- 12 blueberries
- 6 strawberries, sliced
- 1 banana, sliced

NEED DAIRY-FREE? Try a non-dairy cream cheese or spread.

WHAT YOU DO

1. Spread a thin layer of cream cheese onto your rice crackers.
2. Place 1 or 2 blueberries in the middle of each rice cracker.
3. Arrange the sliced strawberries and bananas around the blueberries, like petals on a flower. Enjoy!

ASK AN ADULT TO HELP YOU!

Sudoku Bake Off!

Help Malibu and Brooklyn doodle these yummy snacks into the grids, so there is only one of each item in every row and column.

Answers on page 69.

GROUP CHAT!

Tell Brooklyn and Malibu three things you love to bake or eat.

Vacay Vibes

Can you fit all the dream holidays into the grid below?

sightseeing

camping

diving

beach

adventures

skiing

safari

hiking

cruise

d ... g   h
         k
   s   a   m
t
c   i
g   s   g
         h

Answers on page 69.

WHAT KIND OF HOLIDAY
DO YOU DREAM OF?
☐ Winter sports
☐ Beach
☐ Cruise
☐ Adventures
☐ Sightseeing
☐ Diving

24

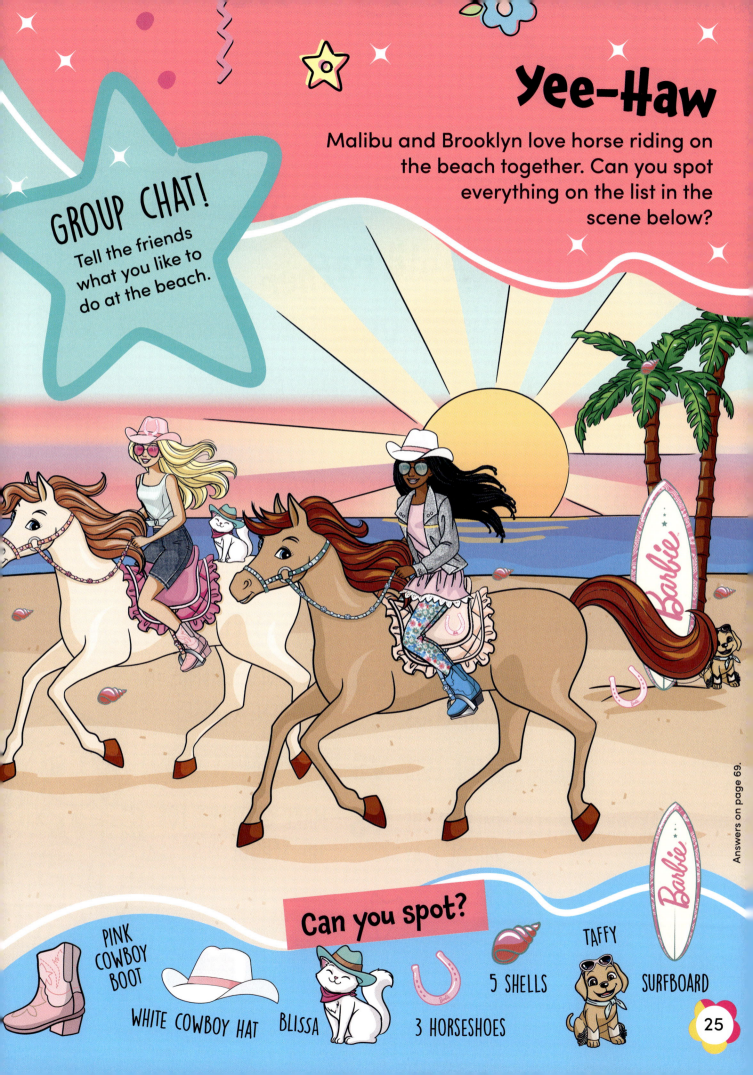

Yee-Haw

Malibu and Brooklyn love horse riding on the beach together. Can you spot everything on the list in the scene below?

GROUP CHAT!
Tell the friends what you like to do at the beach.

Can you spot?

PINK COWBOY BOOT

WHITE COWBOY HAT

BLISSA

3 HORSESHOES

5 SHELLS

TAFFY

SURFBOARD

Answers on page 69.

Aim High!

Brooklyn and Malibu want to hear all about what you like to do at school. Circle an answer to the questions below.

I would rather ...

SOLVE A MATHS PROBLEM **VS** GET LOST IN A GOOD BOOK.

EXPERIMENT IN A SCIENCE LAB **VS** PAINT A PICTURE.

RUN IN A RELAY RACE **VS** COMPETE IN A SWIMMING RACE.

LEARN TO PLAY A MUSICAL INSTRUMENT **VS** LEARN TO SPEAK A NEW LANGUAGE.

EAT SCHOOL DINNERS **VS** TAKE A PACKED LUNCH.

LEARN ABOUT VOLCANOES **VS** LEARN ABOUT AMAZING INVENTIONS.

BE WITH THE SAME FRIENDS IN EVERY CLASS **VS** MAKE NEW FRIENDS IN DIFFERENT CLASSES.

JOIN A DRAMA CLUB **VS** TAKE A DANCE CLASS.

BE THE STAR PERFORMER IN THE SCHOOL PLAY **VS** MAKE COSTUMES FOR THE SCHOOL PLAY.

GROUP CHAT!

Tell Brooklyn and Malibu which three subjects you like best at school.

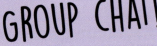

26

School Awards

Brooklyn and Malibu admire all their school friends – each one is special in their own way. Fill in the names of your friends and classmates for the awards below.

Chattiest:
_____

Hardest working:
_____

Friendliest:
_____

Funniest:
_____

Sportiest:
_____

Most dramatic:
_____

Most adventurous:
_____

Kindest:
_____

Most musical:
_____

Barbie
A TOUCH OF MAGIC

A DATE TO Remember

PART ONE

"oh no! I'm in such big trouble!"

"We just have to keep Peggy safe"

1

Rocki, a magical being from Mesmer, was in California searching for Peggy, the baby pegasus. But the Glyph Council, who were in charge of Mesmer, wanted her to come back.

2

Meanwhile, Malibu and Brooklyn discussed Peggy. She was about to grow wings and when that happened, she would have the power to grant the most powerful wish. But according to an old book, someone wanted to steal that wish ...

"Look! It's the Glyph from the book."

3

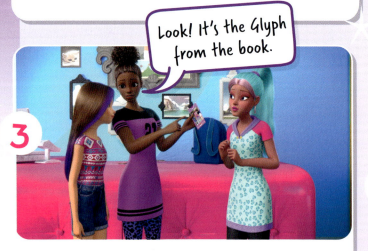

Brooklyn and Skipper decided to go and look for the wish thief. They stopped at the Selfie Museum and spotted flyers with a picture of some Glyphs from Mesmer. One of them looked suspiciously like Rocki.

"Do you know these girls?"

4

Skipper recognised the top that one of the Glyphs was wearing. She took Brooklyn to the shop that sold them. "I know them," the shop assistant said. "They hang out at the juice bar."

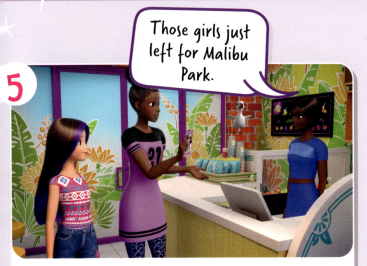

5 The girls set off for the juice bar. "They just left here," the shop owner told them. They would never find them at this rate!

6 Meanwhile, Malibu and Ken arrived at the Selfie Museum. It was their first date and Malibu was nervous. She headed to the bathroom.

7 But in a storage room next to the bathroom, Rocki was transforming into a Glyph. "I just need a spell to help me reach the Glyph Council," mumbled Rocki.

8 Just then, the door swung open and Malibu walked in, thinking she had found the bathroom. "You!" Malibu shouted when she spotted Rocki.

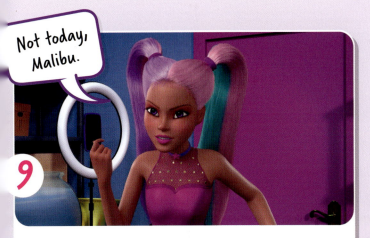

9 "Me! You can't see me here. FOOORGET!" said Rocki, snapping her fingers and pushing Malibu back through the door.

10 Now Malibu was lost. "Where am I? It looks like the Selfie Museum," she said to herself, as she walked back towards Ken.

11

Soon, Malibu spotted Ken. "Good, you made it," she smiled. "Huh?" Ken replied, feeling confused. He took Malibu's hand and led her to the sushi set. But Malibu remembered she needed the bathroom. "Uh ... didn't you just go?" Ken asked. Mistaking the storage room for the bathroom again, Malibu walked in on Rocki performing another spell.

12

Rocki was not happy to see Malibu. "Yes, I'm her, and I'm a Glyph, and I'm gonna do a much stronger spell this time! SUPER FORGET!" yelled Rocki.

13

Malibu left the storage room once more but this time she was even more confused. "Ken? What are you doing here?" she asked. Now Ken went with Malibu to see what was going on.

14

"You!" said Malibu. "Yes, ME!" replied the Glyph. "Who are you, and why are you at the Selfie Museum?" Malibu asked. Before the Glyph could answer, Brooklyn and Skipper walked in.

15

"What's going on in here?"

"Are you two finally on a date?" asked Brooklyn. "We need to focus," replied Malibu. All of a sudden, Rocki cried "MEGA FORGET!" and snapped her fingers.

16

How did we get here? I don't remember a thing.

There was a flash of light as the four friends got hit by a blast of magic and Rocki disappeared. Then they all stumbled out into the museum.

Do you know this girl?

17

Later, two girls came into the museum. Brooklyn recognised them – they were the ones from the flyer. "Do you know this girl?" Brooklyn asked them, pointing at a photo of the Glyph. The girls shook their heads.

18

The friends felt totally lost. "Why do I feel like I'm forgetting something really important?" Brooklyn asked. "Maybe because you are? I think I am too," Ken replied, feeling confused.

The story continues on page 44.

Dreamcatcher

Follow the steps below to create this fun dreamcatcher and help make your dreams come true.

WHAT YOU NEED

- Scissors
- Glue
- Thin card, e.g. cereal box
- Hole punch
- Thread or ribbon
- Other accessories, e.g. beads and feathers

WHAT YOU DO

1. Remove the opposite page and choose which side you'd like for your dreamcatcher. Glue the other side to some thin card, you could use an old cereal box.

2. Ask an adult to help you cut along the dotted lines, so you have two circles.

3. Carefully use a hole punch to punch holes where **a** marks the spot.

4. Take some coloured thread or ribbon and weave it in and out of the holes marked **a** to join the two circles together. Secure it in place with a small knot.

5. Use the hole punch to punch holes where **b** marks the spot. Take some more thread or ribbon and attach three 5cm lengths to the three holes at the bottom of your dreamcatcher. You could thread some beads and feathers onto this dangling thread.

6. Finally, punch a hole where **c** marks the spot and attach some thread or ribbon to the top hole to create a loop. Now you can hang your dreamcatcher over your bed!

ASK AN ADULT TO HELP YOU!

DREAM BIG

Did you know?

DREAMCATCHERS ARE SAID TO CATCH BAD DREAMS IN THEIR NET, BUT LET THE GOOD DREAMS PASS THROUGH.

DREAM BIG

© Mattel.

GROUP CHAT!

Tell Brooklyn and Malibu about the best dream you've ever had.

34

Little Jar of Joy

Follow the simple steps to make little jars of happiness for you and your bestie.

WHAT YOU NEED

- Strips of paper
- Pen or pencil for writing
- 2 clean and empty glass jars with lids (e.g. jam jar)
- Glass marker pens, paint, ribbon or washi tape to decorate your jars
- Scissors

WHAT YOU DO

1. Write messages, jokes, ideas or encouraging notes on your strips of paper. You could decorate them with drawings and add some colour!

2. Fold up the strips of paper and divide them between the two jars.

3. Decorate your jars with little doodles, or wrap some ribbon or washi tape around them for decoration.

4. Give one jar to your BFF and keep one for yourself.

5. Every time you and your friend are in need of a little pick-me-up, do a lucky dip in the jar and pull out an idea, joke or quote to brighten your day.

HERE ARE SOME IDEAS OF WHAT YOU COULD WRITE!

Focus on the good!

If you can dream it, you can do it!

Adventure awaits!

ASK AN ADULT TO HELP YOU!

Dream Home

Let your creativity run wild and create your perfect dream house by ticking the boxes below.

STYLE OF HOME

- ☐ shiny and modern
- ☐ traditional design
- ☐ wild and wacky
- ☐ cool, calming colours
- ☐ bright rainbow colours
- ☐ black and white

TYPE OF HOME

- ☐ mansion
- ☐ city flat
- ☐ beach house
- ☐ loft apartment
- ☐ tree house
- ☐ camper van
- ☐ country cottage

HOW MANY ROOMS?

☐ 3   ☐ 5   ☐ 10   ☐ 20

LOCATION

- ☐ close to a lake or river
- ☐ near lots of shops
- ☐ near cinema/theatre
- ☐ close to my friends
- ☐ close to my family
- ☐ in a forest
- ☐ in a foreign country
- ☐ by the sea

SPECIAL FEATURES

- [ ] movie room
- [ ] swimming pool
- [ ] gym
- [ ] dance studio
- [ ] walk-in wardrobe
- [ ] secret library
- [ ] pet zone
- [ ] games room

Now doodle your dream house!

Perfect Patterns

Can you help Malibu work out what comes next in these patterns? Doodle the answers.

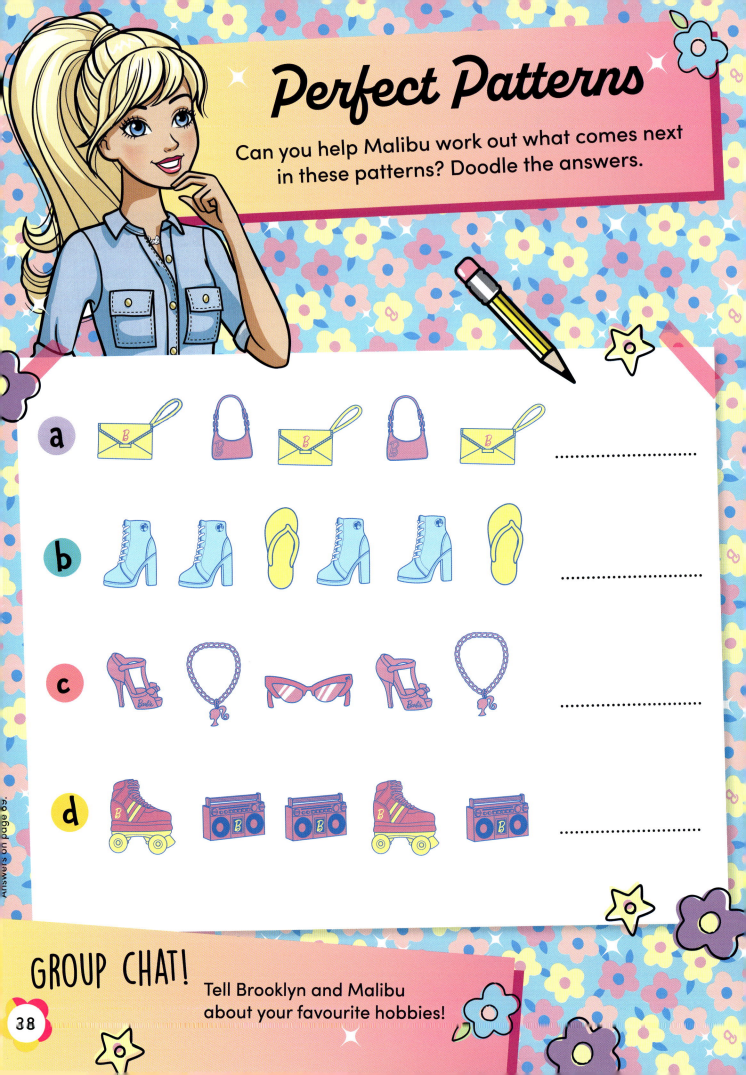

a ....

b ....

c ....

d ....

Answers on page 69.

GROUP CHAT!

Tell Brooklyn and Malibu about your favourite hobbies!

Holly Jolly Vibes

Brooklyn, Malibu and Daisy are sharing Christmas gifts with each other. Follow the ribbons to see what they have received!

JUMPER

DAISY

MALIBU

BROOKLYN

HAT

SNOW GLOBE

Answers on page 69.

Pawsome Pets

Do you dream of owning a meow-vellous kitty or fur-bulous hamster? Take this quick quiz to find the perfect pet for you!

WOULD YOU LIKE A FURRY PET?

YES

NO

DO YOU WANT A PET THAT NEEDS A LOT OF EXERCISE?

WOULD YOU LIKE A PET THAT LIVES IN WATER?

YES

NO

NO

YES

DO YOU WANT TO TRAIN YOUR PET TO DO TRICKS?

WOULD YOU LIKE YOUR PET TO FLY?

YES

NO

YES

NO

DO YOU WANT A PET THAT CAN LIVE OUTSIDE?

WOULD YOU LIKE AN UNUSUAL PET THAT NOT MANY PEOPLE HAVE?

YES

NO

YES

NO

Dog

Rabbit

Bird

Turtle

Cat

Hamster

Lizard

Goldfish

Animal Magic

Malibu and Brooklyn love volunteering at the vets. Can you help them match these pet pictures into pairs? Watch out, one pet doesn't have a match!

Answers on page 69.

GROUP CHAT! Tell Brooklyn and Malibu if you're a cat person or a dog person. Or both!

Love the Game

Find a friend to play this fun game. Take turns drawing one horizontal or vertical line between two dots. The goal is to create a box. Each time you complete a box, mark it with your initials.

Scores:

PLADER 1 ....

PLAYER 2 ....

An empty box = 1 point

A box with a 👟 in = 2 points

A box with a 🏀 in = 3 points

When all boxes have been completed, add up your score. The player with the most points wins!

42

Goal Getter

Close your eyes and see if you can draw a line from Barbie and her friends' footballs into the goal.

Answers on page 69.

WHAT'S THE SCORE?

How many times can you spot the word BALL in the grid below? Look up, down, forwards, backwards and diagonally.

B	A	L	L	B
A	B	L	A	L
B	A	L	L	L
L	L	A	B	A
B	L	B	L	B

Barbie
A TOUCH OF MAGIC
Tiny
PART TWO PROBLEMS
Continued from A Date to Remember ...

1

"I'll bring you Peggy."

With a flash of light, Rocki appeared back in Mesmer. But the Glyph Council leader was not happy with her. "I will forgive you for leaving Mesmer if you bring us the Pegasus," she told Rocki.

2

"Glyphs believe anything you tell them!"

When the Glyph Council leader finished talking to Rocki, she snuck away to a secret cave and transformed into a lizard. Rocki had been tricked!

3

"Your wings are on their way."

Meanwhile, the girls were brushing Peggy when they found another feather. "She's getting more every day," said Brooklyn, excitedly. She put the feather in her pocket.

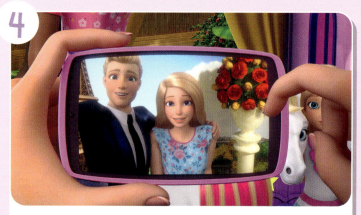

4

Malibu grabbed her phone to take a photo. But when she opened her app, a picture of her with Ken appeared. "How do I not remember this?" wondered Malibu.

5 "Ken has been acting a bit odd," said Malibu. They go to the Selfie Museum to ask Rocki if she remembers seeing them there.

6 When they found Rocki, they suddenly felt suspicious. "Hang on, you're a ... Glyph!" said Brooklyn. With that, Rocki shrank them.

7 Rocki shut tiny Malibu and Brooklyn into a doll's house to keep them out of the way, with her pet duck Tiger keeping watch. Just then, Malibu spotted something.

8 "Look. That feather ... it's from Peggy!" cried Malibu. "Which means Rocki is the one after Peggy's wish!" said Brooklyn.

9 Rocki snuck off to find Peggy. She told Skipper she was a talent scout, tricking her way into the Dreamhouse.

10 As soon as Tiger fell asleep, the girls escaped to phone Skipper on Malibu's phone, which had fallen on the floor.

11

When Skipper picked up, all she could hear was the tiny friends squeaking. "I have NO idea what you're saying," replied Skipper, "but I've got to go with Rocki to the beach." Malibu tried her best to warn Skipper, but it was no good. "Don't go!" Malibu and Brooklyn squeaked together. But the squeaking woke up Tiger – who started chasing them!

12

At the beach, Skipper was busy setting up her DJ gear for the audition. Whenever Peggy saw Rocki, she looked very worried.

13

The girls were hiding from Tiger when Malibu noticed Brooklyn's pocket glowing. It was Peggy's feather from earlier! "It senses the one in the little house," said Malibu.

14

While Brooklyn distracted Tiger, Malibu took the feather into the little house. She held it next to the other one and made a wish. "Here goes. I wish we were big again," she said.

Back to their normal size, Malibu and Brooklyn looked down at Tiger. "No more trouble from you today," said Malibu. Tiger quickly flew away!

At the beach, a crowd had gathered for Skipper's DJ set. Just then, Malibu and Brooklyn arrived to find Peggy.

But Rocki had led Peggy to the far end of the beach. "I'm the key to your mission," Rocki told Peggy. "Come with me, and we both get what we want." Suddenly, Rocki snapped her fingers and said, "Reveal!" With this, a boat appeared.

Malibu and Brooklyn were still searching the beach when they spotted a strange boat heading out to sea. "Rocki's getting away ... with Peggy!" cried Malibu.

The story continues on page 62.

Secret Keeper

Follow the steps below to create a code wheel for you and your bestie, to keep your secrets safe.

WHAT YOU NEED

- Scissors
- 2 split pins

WHAT YOU DO

1. Ask an adult to help you cut out all the wheels on the opposite page.

2. Place a small circle on top of a big circle and carefully push a split pin through the centre to join them together.

3. Spin the smaller circle to a position where the letters are incorrectly aligned.

4. Choose one pair of letters so you can remember the position of the wheel – this is your cipher, e.g. M = B (Malibu = Brooklyn). Make sure you don't forget it!

5. Write a short sentence, encoding it by using the smaller circle letters instead of the larger circle letters.

6. Give a code wheel to a friend, along with your cipher (e.g. M = B) and see if your friend can decode your message.

ASK AN ADULT
TO HELP YOU!

49

GROUP CHAT! Tell Brooklyn and Malibu a secret about yourself!

Makeover Time

Colour in the clothes and accessories to create a fabulous fashion wardrobe!

NOW DOODLE SOME FUN ACCESSORIES BELOW. MAYBE SOME COOL SHADES OR A NECKLACE?

Adventure Awaits

Barbie, Ken and Renee are off to skate with their friends. Who will reach the skate park? Whose path will lead them to a puppy? Who will not get to the park at all?

BARBIE

KEN

RENEE

SKATE PARK

Answers on page 69.

Trailblazers

Barbie and her friends love horse riding!
Can you spot 5 differences between the pictures below?

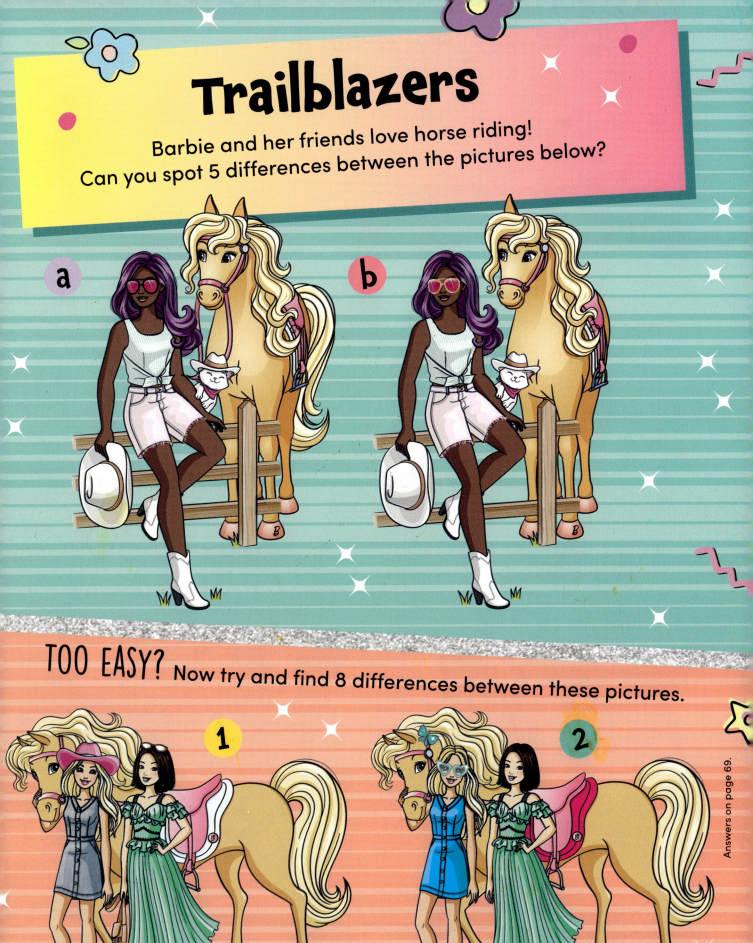

a

b

TOO EASY? Now try and find 8 differences between these pictures.

1

2

Answers on page 69.

Cluedunnit?

Can you follow the clues to see who baked a surprise treat of donuts for their friends?

The kind friend is wearing lace-up shoes.

The mystery baker is not wearing sunglasses.

This person has an 'r' in their name.

DAISY

TERESA

MALIBU

Answers on page 69.

The mystery donut baker is:

54

NOW USE THE CLUES BELOW TO REVEAL WHICH MISCHIEF-MAKING PET LEFT THE TRAIL OF MUDDY PAWPRINTS.

She is not wearing pink.

RENEE

BROOKLYN

1

2

3

4

5

The naughty pet is a dog.

This pawsome pet is wearing a collar.

The mystery mutt is not wearing sunglasses.

This canine cutie is wearing a pink bow.

The mystery messy pet is:

....

Hello Universe!

Find a friend and join Malibu and Brooklyn on a cosmic adventure in this fun game. All you need is a dice and coins for counters.

START

1

2 MAKE A WISH ON A SHOOTING STAR AND HAVE ANOTHER GO.

3

4

19

18

17

16 TRUE OR FALSE? THE SUN IS A STAR. GET IT RIGHT AND MOVE FORWARD 3 SPACES.

15

20 OOPS! YOU LOST A SPACE BOOT. GO BACK TO THE START.

21

22

23

Barbie WINS!

10

11

12 FUEL UP ON POPCORN AND ZOOM ON 1 SPACE.

13

14

9

8 TRUE OR FALSE? EARTH TRAVELS AROUND THE SUN. GET IT RIGHT AND HAVE ANOTHER GO.

7

6

5

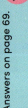
Answers on page 69.

Choose to play as Malibu or Brooklyn and place your coin counters on their starting spaces. Take it in turns to roll the dice and move your coin counters through the spaces.

Follow the instructions on the spaces as you go. The first player to reach their planet WINS.

= fly on 2 spaces.

= go back 3 spaces.

5

6 STOP TO REFUEL YOUR ROCKET AND MISS A GO.

7

8

9 NAME THE PLANET WE LIVE ON. GET IT RIGHT AND MOVE ON 1 SPACE.

14

13

12

11 IS THE MILKY WAY A GALAXY OR AN ASTEROID? GET IT RIGHT AND HAVE ANOTHER GO.

10

Barbie WINS!

23

22

21

20 OOPS! YOU DROPPED A SPACE GLOVE, GO BACK TO THE START.

15 WHICH PLANET HAS RINGS: JUPITER OR SATURN? GET IT RIGHT AND ZOOM ON 3 SPACES.

16

17

18

19 HOW MANY PLANETS ARE IN OUR SOLAR SYSTEM? GET IT RIGHT AND HAVE ANOTHER GO.

4

3

2

1

START

Share Together

Check out these fun friendship-building games and activities to play with your besties.

Trust Walker

(4 PLAYERS OR MORE)

1. Divide your group into teams, with two players on each team.

2. Create an obstacle course for each team with chairs, tables and toys you have at home.

3. One player puts on a blindfold. The other player will be their guide and help them get through the obstacle course by telling them to go over, under and around things.

4. If the blindfolded player bumps into any objects, they must go back to the start.

5. The first team to reach the end of their obstacle course wins.

Ask an adult to help move furniture and check there are no sharp edges before you begin!

Doodle Doubles

(4 PLAYERS OR MORE)

1. Divide the players into two teams, each with two players.

2. One player on each team doodles an animal or object, but should not show their drawing to their teammate.

3. Then, they have to describe their drawing so the other player can doodle it, by describing lines and shapes.

4. The teams then reveal their drawings. The team whose drawings look most alike wins!

Guess the Picture

(2 PLAYERS)

1. Player 1 sits or stands in front of a piece of paper with a pencil.

2. Player 2 uses their finger to 'draw' a picture or 'write' a word on Player 1's back.

3. Player 1 has to draw what they think Player 2 has drawn on the piece of paper.

4. Check to see if they've got it right!

Two Truths and a Lie

(AT LEAST 2 PLAYERS)

1. Take it in turns to tell two truths and one lie about yourself. Whoever guesses which statement isn't true, gets a point and goes next.

2. You can play as long as you want, then add up the points to reveal the winner.

Shine Bright

Let your imagination run wild! Tick the boxes to decide what kind of outfits you want, then doodle your fashion designs on Malibu and Brooklyn.

WHERE MIGHT THEY WEAR THEIR OUTFIT?

☐ disco

☐ sports event

☐ outing with friends

☐ walk on the beach

WHAT COLOURS WILL YOU CHOOSE?

☐ warm reds, oranges and yellows

☐ cooler green and blue shades

☐ rainbow brights

☐ black and white

WHAT ACCESSORIES MIGHT GO WITH YOUR OUTFIT DESIGN?

☐ hat
☐ gloves
☐ boots
☐ bag

BARBIE GIRL

GROUP CHAT!

Tell Brooklyn and Malibu what your three favourite colours are.

61

Barbie A TOUCH OF MAGIC

PART THREE

Continued from Tiny Problems ...

LIZARD lift-off

1

You'll never catch us now!

Malibu and Brooklyn watched from the beach as Rocki set off on her magical boat with Peggy. They needed to get her back!

2

Rocki has done something bad.

So, Malibu and Brooklyn jumped straight into Ken's lifeguard boat and chased them. But Rocki was up to her old tricks ...

3

Not so fast.

"Empty-o!" called Rocki.
In no time Ken's boat slowed down.
"Out of fuel already?" giggled Rocki as she watched Ken's boat come to a stop.

4

Look, I've found more fuel, guys!

Brooklyn searched the boat and found a full bottle of fuel. But by the time they were ready to go, Rocki's boat was out of sight.
"Which way now?" sighed Malibu.

5

"Look up there!"

"I'm no expert, but I think following a dragon is a good place to start," said Brooklyn, pointing to the sky.

6

"That way! Follow that boat!"

Trey and Skipper were also chasing after Rocki on Trey's boat. They were pretty lost until Skipper spotted a boat on the horizon.

7

Meanwhile, Rocki's boat was getting nearer to a mysterious island. There was a magical purple fog all around it.

8

"Something isn't right, here."

On the island, Rocki met with The Glyph Council Leader. But something wasn't right. The leader was acting strangely! "Erm, I think we'll leave," said Rocki.

9

"You! What do you want with Peggy?"

But suddenly a cage appeared around Peggy and the leader transformed into a lizard. "You're the evil lizard wizard!" cried Rocki.

10

"I want Peggy's most powerful wish. Duh!"

The lizard told Rocki that he wanted Peggy's first wish after her wings appeared. "The most powerful wish of all," grinned Will, the lizard.

When Rocki tried to set Peggy free, Will set the dragon on her. Luckily, Malibu and Ken arrived just in time! They distracted the dragon so that Rocki could use her magic to free Peggy. "Melt-o!" cried Rocki, and the cage vanished. Brooklyn rushed over to give Peggy a hug.

As soon as Peggy was free, she floated up into the sky. "Look!" said Malibu, pointing up at Peggy. "Peggy is getting her wings!"

Before anyone could admire Peggy's new wings, the friends had to escape the island. They all ran to the boats as fast as they could, only to discover they had vanished.

Rocki tried to cast a spell to get the boats back but nothing happened. "You don't have your powers," called Will. "But I do! And I'm going turn you all into newts ..." he laughed.

15

Barbie is in danger.

At sea, Skipper and Trey reached the boat they'd seen on the horizon. It belonged to a pirate who agreed to help find Barbie.

16

The pirate cast a spell and the trio landed on the island with a bang that blew Will far away. Malibu couldn't believe her eyes!

17

Skip, how did you do that? You're amazing!

It turned out that this pirate was actually the Glyph Council Leader all along. "You are all safe as long as you leave the island," she told them calmly. Everyone was safe and they'd made a new friend in Rocki!

THE END

Splish, Splash, Sparkle!

How quickly can you spot all the things on the list below?
Ready, set ... sparkle!

Can you spot?

2 SEAHORSES

5 STARFISH

1 CONCH SHELL

3 NARWHALS

8 BUBBLES

4 MAGIC WANDS

3 CLAM SHELLS

Answers on page 69.

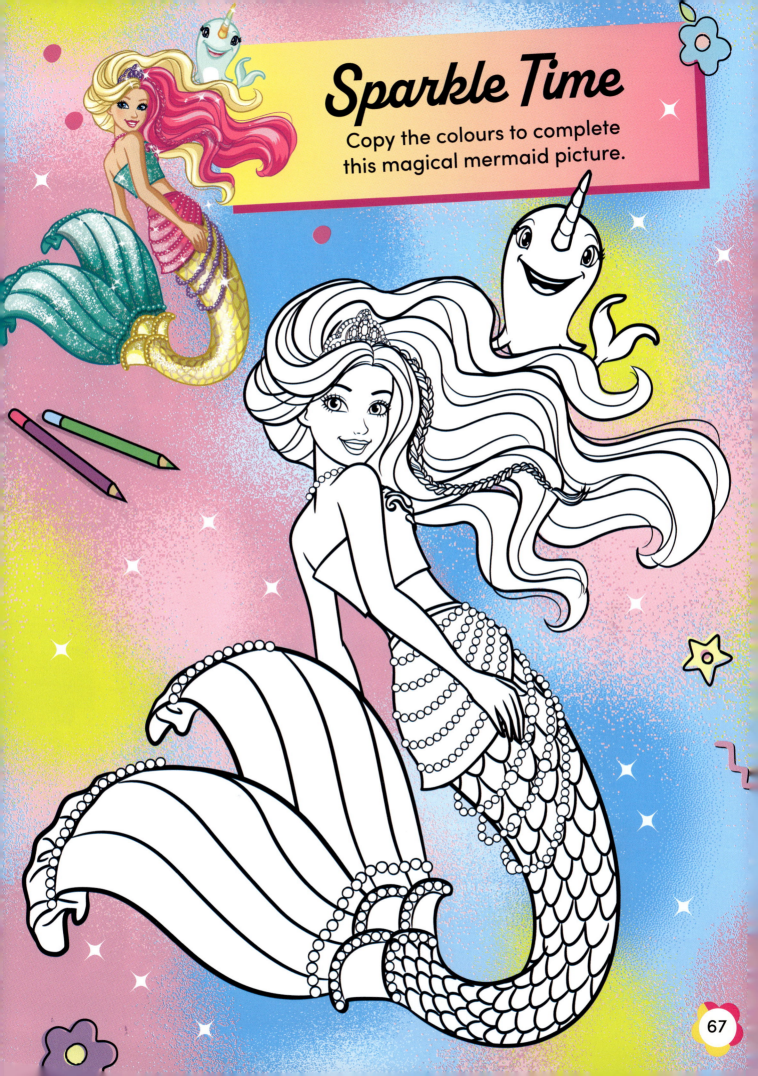

Sparkle Time

Copy the colours to complete this magical mermaid picture.

67

BARBIE

Page 12

Page 13

a. Sunglasses   c. Trainers
b. Backpack   d. Earphones

Page 19

1. c
2. d
3. e
4. b
5. a

Page 20

Renee

Nikki

Daisy

Page 23

Page 24

a
d i v i n g   h i k i n g
v   i   c
e   s a f a r i n g   a
n   k   g   m
t   i   p
u   c r u i s e   i
r   b   n
e   s i g h t s e e i n g
a
c
h

Page 25

Page 38

a.   c.
b.   d.

Page 39

Daisy – Snow globe
Malibu – Jumper
Brooklyn – Hat

Page 41

Page 43

B A L L B
A B L A L
B A L L L
L L A B A
B L B L B

BALL appears
7 times

Page 52

Renee reaches the puppy.
Ken doesn't get to the park.
Barbie reaches the skate park.

Page 53

Page 54–55

The mystery donut baker is Brooklyn.
The mystery messy pet is number 4.

Page 56–57

Malibu
9. Earth
11. Galaxy
16. True

Brooklyn
8. True
15. Saturn
19. Eight

Page 66